THIEVES OF PARADISE

WESLEYAN POETRY

ALSO BY YUSEF KOMUNYAKAA

Dedications & Other Darkhorses (1977)

Lost in the Bonewheel Factory (1979)

Copacetic (1984)

I Apologize for the Eyes in My Head (1986)

Toys in a Field (1986)

Dien Cai Dau (1988)

February in Sydney (1989)

Magic City (1992)

Neon Vernacular (1993)

THIEVES OF PARADISE

Yusef Komunyakaa

Wesleyan University Press

Published by University Press of New England

Hanover and London

FOR MANDY, AGAIN

WESLEYAN UNIVERSITY PRESS

Published by University Press of New England, Hanover, NH 03755

Printed in the United States of America   5   4   3   2

CIP data appear at the end of the book

ACKNOWLEDGMENTS

Grateful acknowledgment is made to the following publications, in which these poems originally appeared: *African-American Review, Agni, The American Poetry Review, Art/Life, The Asian Pacific American Journal, Boulevard, Brilliant Corners, Caliban, Callaloo, Common Knowledge, Crab Orchard Review, Crazyhorse, Field, Fish Stories, The Flying Island, Green Mountains Review, Hayden's Ferry Review, Heartland Today, The Hopewell Review, The Illinois Review, The Iowa Review, Many Mountains Moving, The Massachusetts Review, Michigan Quarterly Review, New England Review, The Occident, The Pacific Review, The Paris Review, The Philadelphia Inquirer, Phoebe, Prosodia, River Styx, Shankpainter, The Southern California Anthology, The Southern Review, TriQuarterly, VOLT.*

"Testimony" was first aired by Australian Broadcasting Corporation, with music composed by Sandy Evans and directed by Chris Williams.

"Ia Drang Valley" first appeared in *The Made Thing: An Anthology of Contemporary Southern Poetry*, University of Arkansas, 1987.

CONTENTS

WAY STATIONS

MEMORY CAVE

A tallow worked into a knot
of rawhide, with a ball of waxy light
tied to a stick, the boy
scooted through a secret mouth
of the cave, pulled by the flambeau
in his hand. He could see
the gaze of agate eyes
& wished for the forbidden
plains of bison & wolf, years
from the fermented honey
& musty air. In the dried
slag of bear & bat guano,
the initiate stood with sleeping
gods at his feet, lost
in the great cloud of their one
breath. Their muzzles craved
touch. How did they learn
to close eyes, to see into
the future? Before the Before:
mammon was unnamed & mist
hugged ravines & hillocks.
The elders would test him
beyond doubt & blood. Mica
lit the false skies where
stalactite dripped perfection
into granite. He fingered
icons sunlight & anatase
never touched. Ibex carved
on a throwing stick, reindeer
worried into an ivory amulet,
& a bear's head. Outside,
the men waited two days
for him, with condor & bovid,
& not in a thousand years
would he have dreamt a woman
standing here beside a man,
saying, "This is as good
as the stag at Salon Noir

& the polka-dotted horses."
The man scribbles *Leo loves*
Angela below the boy's last bear
drawn with manganese dioxide
& animal fat. This is where
sunrise opened a door in stone
when he was summoned to drink
honey wine & embrace a woman
beneath a five-pointed star.
Lying there beside the gods
hefty & silent as boulders,
he could almost remember
before he was born, could see
the cliff from which he'd fall.

OUT THERE THERE BE DRAGONS

Beyond King Ptolemy's dream
outside the broken
girdle of chance, beyond
the Lighthouse of Pharos
in a kingdom of sea turtles,
nothing can inter or outrun
a stormy heart. Beyond galleon
& disappearing lovers, a flame
flounces behind a glass crab
to signal a craggy reef
in the Bay of Alexandria.
Beyond archipelagos of drizzle
& salt, Armageddon & hellfire,
bearded seals turn into Helen's
mermaids sunning on a white beach
beside Paris, where blotches of ink
map omens. Beyond Atlantis
uncovered by desert winds
phantom armies ride against,
necklaces of shark's teeth
adorn virgins. When earth
dilates, the known magnifies
till unknowns tincture silk,
till pomegranates bleed
redemption into soil.
Sirens cry across dark
waters, as anguelle becomes air,
beyond the mapmaker's omphalos
where hydra first mounted Venus.

THE SONG THIEF

　　　　　Up there
in that diorama of morning
light through springtime branches,
how many feathered lifetimes
sifted down through green
leaves, how many wars sprung up
& ended before the cowbird figured out
laws of gravity in Cloudcuckooland,
before the songbird's egg
was nudged from its nest?
Maybe a flock followed a herd
of heifers across a pasture,
pecking wildflower seed
from fresh dung
when the first urge of switcheroo
flashed in their dirt-colored heads.
What nature of creature comforts
taught the unsung cells this art,
this shell game of odds
& percentages in the serpent's leafy
Babylon? Only the cowbird's mating song
fills the air until their young
are ravenous as five
of the seven deadly sins
woven into one.

WET NURSE

The shadow of a hilltop
        halves an acropolis
in the head of a serf's
        descendant. Heimdall's horn
at the gates of Asgard
        pulses beneath prayers
for wealth. April unhinges
        rings in the cottonwood
till sap seethes from each slow
        hour. A sliver of whalebone
slips from the mother's satin corset
        as the dark-skinned nurse
unbuttons her floral blouse
        & unhooks her cheap bra.
The child swallows a lament,
        & his rich father nods
to a reproduction of Da Vinci's
        Madonna Litta to answer
silence, to quieten his fear
        of the primal in the wife's
smile. But what isn't desired
        stays a hard-green or grows
too sweet for the tongue.
        A cry, a wet trigger——
agog. Not enough milk
        left for her own child,
each nipple's an eyedropper
        of rage & beatitude.

ODE TO A DRUM

Gazelle, I killed you
for your skin's exquisite
touch, for how easy it is
to be nailed to a board
weathered raw as white
butcher paper. Last night
I heard my daughter praying
for the meat here at my feet.
You know it wasn't anger
that made me stop my heart
till the hammer fell. Weeks
ago, I broke you as a woman
once shattered me into a song
beneath her weight, before
you slouched into that
grassy hush. But now
I'm tightening lashes,
shaping hide as if around
a ribcage, stretched
like five bowstrings.
Ghosts cannot slip back
inside the body's drum.
You've been seasoned
by wind, dust & sunlight.
Pressure can make everything
whole again, brass nails
tacked into the ebony wood
your face has been carved
five times. I have to drive
trouble from the valley.
Trouble in the hills.
Trouble on the river
too. There's no kola nut,
palm wine, fish, salt,
or calabash. Kadoom.
Kadoom.   Kadooom.   Ka-
doooom.   Kadoom.   Now
I have beaten a song back into you,
rise & walk away like a panther.

ECLOGUE AT DAYBREAK

His unlidded eyes a wish
always coming true,
as his body slithered
from a sheath of skin
half-alive on the grass
like a final lesson on escape.
He moved only when other things
strayed beyond suspicion.
The worlds inside sleep
couldn't hold him. In an arcade
somewhere in a marketplace
he was Houdini reincarnated
in a box. Soon came the hour
he was created for: a woman,
free-footed as Isadora
in sashes, draped his body
over hers. An apprentice
placed an apple in her left hand
& lush gardens sprouted across
three canvases. Her smooth skin,
how his wedge-shaped head
lingered between her breasts,
left him drowsy. The clocks
sped up. A cruel season
fell across their pose
as they began a slow dance.
She reshaped the pattern of skulls
on his yellow skin, a deep
falling inside him when her hips
quivered & arms undulated,
stealing the pleas of prey.

GENEALOGY

We were almost unreal.
      If you don't believe me,
    let the wind open the *Journals*

of the House of Burgesses
      so you can hear it whisper
    lessons of the soil through maple

& birch. We buried
      ourselves in holes, shelter
    we could wrestle free of earth

& wood held in place by snow,
      this last door nailed shut
    with icicles. Rations dwindled

to eight ounces of meal
      & a pint of peas a day,
    working with maggots & cobwebs.

That winter a man salted down guilt,
      feeding upon his wife
    till she was only a head.

You can erase Sir Thomas Smith
      from your genealogical charts;
    our ancestors stole handfuls of oats

& were chained to trees,
      starved or broken
    slowly on the wheel,

& here's our coat of arms.
      This crossbone. This boar
    wreathed with hemlock & laurel.

KOSMOS

Walt, you shanghaied me to this
oak, as every blood-tipped leaf
soliloquized "Strange Fruit"
like the octoroon in New Orleans

who showed you how passion
ignited dogwood, how it rose
from inside the singing sap.
You heard primordial notes

murmur up from the Mississippi,
a clank of chains among the green
ithyphallic totems, betting your heart
could run vistas with Crazy Horse

& runaway slaves. Sunset dock
to whorehouse, temple to hovel,
your lines traversed America's
white space, driven by a train whistle.

*

Believing you could be three places
at once, you held the gatekeeper's daughter,
lured by the hard eyes of his son,
on a voyage in your head

to a face cut into Mount Rushmore.
You knew the curse in sperm
& egg, but had faith in the soil,
that it would work itself out

in generations, springs piercing bedrock.
Love pushed through jailhouses, into bedrooms
of presidents & horse thieves,
oil sucked into machines in sweatshops

& factories. I followed from my hometown

where bedding an oak is bread on the table;
where your books, as if flesh, were locked
in a glass case behind the check-out desk.

*

Wind-jostled foliage—a scherzo,
a bellydancer adorned in bells.
A mulatto moon halved into yesterday
& tomorrow, some balustrade

full-bloomed. But you taught home
was wherever my feet took me,
birdsong over stockyards or Orient,
fused by handshake & blood.

Seed & testament, naked
among fire-nudged thistle,
from the Rockies to below
sea level, to the steamy bayous,

I traipsed your footpath.
Falsehoods big as stumbling blocks
in the mind, lay across the road,
beside a watery swoon.

*

I'm back with the old folk
who speak your glossolalia of pure
sense unfolding one hundred years.
Unlocked chemistry, we're tied to sex,

spectral flower twisted out of
filigreed language & taboo
stubborn as crabgrass. You slept
nude under god-hewn eyes & ears.

Laughter in trees near a canebrake,
I know that song. Old hippie,

before Selma & People's Park,
your democratic nights a vortex

of waterlilies. The skin's cage
opened, but you were locked inside
your exotic Ethiopia. Everything
sprung back like birds after a shot.

CONFLUENCE

I've been here before, dreaming myself
backwards, among grappling hooks of light.

True to the seasons, I've lived every word
spoken. Did I walk into someone's nightmare?

Hunger quivers on a fleshy string
at the crossroad. So deep in the lore,

there's only tomorrow today where darkness
splinters & wounds the bird of paradise.

On paths that plunge into primordial
green, Echo's laughter finds us together.

In the sweatshops of desire men think
if they don't die the moon won't rise.

All the dead-end streets run into one
moment of bliss & sleight of hand.

Beside the Euphrates, past the Tigris,
up the Mississippi. Bloodline & clockwork.

The X drawn where we stand. Trains
follow rivers that curve around us.

The distant night opens like a pearl
fan, a skirt, a heart, a drop of salt.

When we embrace, we are not an island
beyond fables & the blue exhaust of commerce.

When the sounds of River Styx punish
trees, my effigy speaks to the night owl.

Our voices break open the pink magnolia
where struggle is home to the beast in us.

All the senses tuned for the Hawkesbury,
labyrinths turning into lowland fog.

Hand in hand, feeling good, we walk
phantoms from the floating machine.

When a drowning man calls out,
his voice follows him downstream.

PALIMPSEST

Modern Medea

Apex, triangle . . . a dead child
on the floor between his mother
& four slavecatchers in a Cincinnati hideout.
Blood colors her hands

& the shadow on the wall
a lover from the grave.
She sacrificed her favorite
first. He must've understood,

stopped like a stone figure.
Where's the merciful weapon, sharp
as an icepick or hook knife?
We know it was quick,

a stab of light. Treed
as if by dogs around an oak—
she stands listening to a river
sing, begging salt for her wounds.

Meditations on a Smoothing Iron

They touched fingers to tongues,
& then tapped you with wet kisses.
You've outlasted five women
who pressed white shirts of bankers,

preachers, bartenders, & thieves.
You left an imprint on a pair of trousers
when he pulled her away & embraced her.
You smoothed the silk underwear

of a thirteen-year-old who died
in childbirth. You're the weapon
Three Fingers was done in with.
McGrory wiped off every smudge.

You left Memphis, headed for Ohio,
pushed by hard times. For thirty years
you were a doorstop, & then a Saturday-morning
yardsale made you a debutante's paperweight.

Basiliqué

I dip a twig into a glass of rosé
& the daughter of that Alabama judge
struts through the door,
Rene Depestre. The dead rise

when gods bend me into this
Yanvalou, & nightbirds
sing in the redbuds.
There's no medicine

to cure her of me.
No lies to cut the potion.
I am Papa-Legba
from the backwoods,

& the cock's blood
metamorphoses my hands
into five-pointed stars
holding down the night.

Mercy

Old Lady Emma's calling her dog
Pepper again. I can see skidmarks
where somebody's car tried to brake.
Her voice a high-pitched reed flute.

All day she sings out his name,
but he can't rise from where
I stamped down the red clay.
Can't push away the creek-polished stones.

I told her some boy
from The Projects walked off
with Pepper, that he's bound
to break free & come home.

Leaning on her oak-limb
cane, she wants me to go search
the neighborhood. It'll take half the night
to walk up & down the streets, calling.

Diorama

Terra incognita—crosshairs
& lines on the atlas—anywhere
have-nots outnumber raintrees along avenues
igniting skylines, marrying the dead

to the unborn. The meek. The brain
an Orwellian timemachine where *Boyz
N the Hood* drifts into a Fagin school.
They look for Wild Maggie Carson,

Crazy Butch, the Little Dead Rabbits,
Plug Uglies, & Daylight Boys. No one
escapes the concentric shotgun blast.
Circles reach back to Hell's Kitchen

& out to Dorchester, coldcocking
the precious sham of neon. The night
sways like a pinball machine on a warped floor
slowdragged smooth by Love & Hate in each other's arms.

Red Dust

Gargoyled angels ride
the backs of black men
who hurl their bodies
on exploding grenades,

who vaporize into unquestioned
mist & syllables of names,
who rise like curses & prayers
entwined in broken earth

& fall into smoky-red
cerecloth. An answer

coils around wounded branches.
After fragments of bone

settle on leaves, & birds
reclaim their songs, the world
moves again. Someone speaks
& the army ants go to work.

Descendants of the Dragon

Tanks push till day breaks from night
in Tiananmen Square, as gardens uproot
& bleed a map only the blind follow. The dead
hold each other in broken arms like a fire-gutted

rock 'n' roll dancehall. Chrysanthemum
& lotus take root again, womb to earth,
until human & animal wail as one
outside The Forbidden City.

A line of students falls
beneath a dancing paper dragon. Spent
ammo casings refract lodestone. Flames
push aside a river of voices & singe

trees along The Bamboo Curtain.
Somewhere a seismograph knows now is
the time to drop a bronze ball
into the frog's mouth.

Shape & Sound

Mallets ring out over the Hawkesbury
as they teach stone to worship human posture,
how to be one with hold & abandonment. Below
Wondabyne's sculpture garden a one-carriage railway

crouches in the thigh of the valley. A whistle cuts
like a blade, & the twelve sentinels of Gosford quiver
as commuters wave. Curses have fallen where hands
from Katmandu use two SRA nails to sign the air.

Sculptors from Papua New Guinea, Bulgaria, Nepal,
France, stand with Aussies at the Gateway of Peace.
The song of iron & wood persuades a seven-ton block
to grow into a woman who calls out to passing boats,

a new friend embraced into the world. The stone
figures listen to river music like hands fashioning
lovers in dark curves—in the right angle of a Greek
dead on the ground.

Gutbucket

I'm back, armed
with Muddy's mojo hand.
Take your daughters & hide them.
Redbuds cover the ground

like Lady Day's poppies
kissed beyond salvation & damnation:
so pretty in their Easter dresses
this day of the flower eater.

I'm fool enough to believe
loneliness can never tango me into
oblivion again. I've swayed to Lockjaw,
Trane, Pepper, & Ornette,

& outlived the cold whiteness
of Head Power in Shinjuku.
I know if you touch beauty right
a bird sings the monkey to you.

A Call from the Terrace

Old bile in young fruit
puckers the mouth shut.
Her voice on the phone: *I see you
sometimes from our window*

*when you're grafting roses.
I bet you can't guess*

what my left hand's doing now?
Faces you've known forever

glide by like jack-o'-lanterns,
living to make your life miserable,
kissing pedigreed dogs & cats to sleep
behind padlocked doors.

Inheritors pace-off stolen land.
The dead fertilize the interminable
future, flowers drawing psychosis
up through their roots.

Pain Merchant

Twelve blues songs
distilled, every
letdown focused through eyes
looking into mine. Pestilence

clusters at the base of the spine
the way a tumor flowers. An owl
laments. Each breath takes me back
to the Nile. I am the last stonemason

in Khufu's chamber, locking out
daylight & greed, just before
ascending. I taste each breath.
What did I do to be so black & blue?

fades. I don't care what you say,
with your bright pills & capsules,
I am going to teach Mr. Pain
to sway, to bop.

In Love with The Nightstalker

To kiss death, to sleep
with a persona,
to make love
to Satan & his square-jawed effigies

smiling from *Esquire* & *GQ*.
His double profile in a bedroom mirror:
Crescent, knife in a father's hand.
With so much fear, there's no

orgasm. The brain: a cruel king
ogles from a stone tower.
Or, a dog goes down
on all fours,

crawling in the dust. I stop
& wag my tail. Whining for bread
held out in his left hand, I come forth,
eyes fixed on his right fist cocked like a hammer.

Note to Pavese

I'm in the corner of your right
eye, that black man in a bar
drinking your lush red wine.
As your dream women pass before us,

this one beauty floats into night
mystery—*la donna dalla voce rauca*.
A dress so bright, the place darkens
like a headless rooster across the floor.

Maybe flesh wasn't made to possess.
Sure as Hannibal jostled stone gates,
if you're Mediterranean, Africa sings
in your blood & sperm. Late nights,

as you translated Melville & Faulkner,
did classic fear crawl into you? I don't
know why she came nude to the door, why
she said we'd been making love for days.

Russian Phantasia

The lovers fall asleep after a fifth
of vodka, watching reruns of *Dallas*,

Fantasy Island, & *I Led Three Lives.*
The night's punched black & blue.

Now, they can see Pushkin's
love-sick Evgeny in Petrograd
the moment the Neva leaps
its banks, can hear him cursing

& shaking a balled fist
at Peter the Great's statue.
The bronze horse springs
like an acetylene torch.

They're with Evgeny, caught-up
in the plot, but even ghosts are forbidden
to venture down into catacombs
like ghettoes fenced-in by freeways.

The Modern World

The mind tortures a traitor.
You want to daydream hummingbirds
in larkspur, but all you can see
is the bitch eating her puppies

under the house. You're unsure
if Honey loves you a year later.
The mirrors face each other
so she falls into your arms

when you push her away.
Snow fills the hourglass
as you read Mandelstam's letters
to Gorky about clothes. Be thankful

you whisper. Another bomb-shaped
question glides overhead like the
Hindenburg. You load the gun
when you think you're unloading it.

Nighthawks

Dusk lit paths quicker
than stars on gunmetal. Swift
as bats condemned to dart through
the mind's blue hoops. Smooth

as a boy's flashy hands over a girl's
boyish hips. Shirley Ruth & I knew
where to find each other, hugging
the ground in a place ghosts hid.

Our brothers counted us out
as we kissed under branches of a fig
tree huddled into a wide skirt
against summer grass. Night-

hawks scissored in & out of pines
& oaks, as if pulling silver thread
through a black cloth of loopholes,
a drunk's signature on a quitclaim deed.

Triangles

It's one of those things.
Like drawing a line in the dust
& pointing a chicken's beak
to it. How the hypnosis

works, I don't know.
It's like placing three pans
of dog food on the floor
equally apart.

Triangles are torture.
The dog is condemned
to walk in a circle
till he drops dead.

This is Dante's first cycle,
rings looped inside each other

like a sorcerer's bracelet, a heart
divided into trinity by good & evil.

Balance

I kill a part
so the other lives;
unlike the snake
chopped in half,

rejoining itself among
nightshade. Otherworldly
green—amazed by what
logic weaves as one—

how the sky's balanced
by the ground underfoot.
I think of Count Basie,
what he knew

to leave out. Leverage
determines the arc,
& everything else is
naked grace.

MUMBLE PEG

We stood in a wide-legged
dare, three country boys
triangulating a circle
in April, lines scored in clay.
With the snap of a wrist
bright-handled knives spun
& pierced each other's plot.
Tied to earth, we couldn't run
for the snowball wagon
anymore. The blades marked
our places, as we swaggered
toward the old man
hunched over his metal scoop
singing across the block of ice.
His row of bottles huddled
in slots like a rainbow
under the canopy, & he'd grab
the right flavor without looking,
as if his body didn't need a mind
to guide it. After the sweet air
wore off, we returned to our knives
to homestead spring. Dragonflies
stitched the day with a blue-
green blur. Like Pascal
tossing a coin into the air,
our bodies posed questions
while girls skipped rope
till clay hardened into reddish stone.
They leapt so high they answered
the day as we stood in the silent
council of our pocketknives.
If a boy could no longer stand
like a one-legged crane on the land he owned,
he lost it all. But the winner
always looked the loneliest
in his circle at sunset.
If no one could see us
as the brain divided hemispheres

in the garden, what would we own?
A faint Venus burned the sky
as we bet each girl a kiss
if we guessed the color of her underwear.

IA DRANG VALLEY

To sleep here, I play dead.
My mind takes me over the Pacific
to my best friend's wife nude
on their bed. I lean over
& kiss her. Sometimes the spleen
decides what it takes to bridge
another night. The picture
dissolves into gray as I fight,
cussing the jumpcut that pulls me back
to the man in a white tunic,
where I'm shoved against the wall
with the rest of the hostages.
The church spire hides
under dusk in the background,
& my outflung arms shadow bodies
in the dirt. I close my eyes
but Goya's *Third of May* holds
steady, growing sharper. I stand
before the bright rifles,
nailed to the moment.

CENOTAPH

An owl hoots my dead friend's name
from a high branch, gossiping
about how I dreamt his sister
nude beside me in Chu Lai,
how sometimes their faces
were one. I can't escape
his voice & her onyx eyes
montaged into a hot season.
Maybe she'd see Judas
if we embraced. Or believe
she's hugging her brother,
kissing him back into this world.
Denial is a cardinal flying backwards,
as if the ambush were shooting stars
along a paddie dike. Blackberries
color our lips. The times we played
Buffalo Bill & Sitting Bull,
he'd fall like a shadow in a cenotaph,
but my teasing never failed to raise
his eyelids. I know his mother
tried to pull the flag to the floor
& pry open the coffin. There's no verb
to undo the night he hit the booby trap,
& I know shame would wear me like a mask
against a century of hot morning light
if I didn't slowdrag to Rockin' Dopsie.

THE TRAPPER'S BRIDE

She's from Bengal or Kashmir,
holding James Dean's hand
in *East of Eden.* I wonder
if I'm a eunuch in her head,
as we face this Indian warrior
selling his daughter for guns,
red flannel, beads, tobacco,
& blankets. The green sky
& pale horse counterpoint
the bride's bemusement.
What about the other woman
half nude on the ground
in a red garment, like hush
& rage brushed over primer?
The trappers sit like Jesus
& a shepherd in rawhide,
years from their future
on a hill of buffalo skulls
at Michigan Carbon Works.
We survey the vista of golds
& dark accents. She says, "Oops,"
when our eyes meet, as she leans
forward in a lowcut blouse, almost
touching the canvas. Yes,
he knew how to work with light.
A bruise seethes into the lost
colors of our mute rendezvous.

ECLOGUE AT TWILIGHT

The three wrestle in the grass
five or ten minutes, shaking blooms
& winged seeds to the ground.
The lioness lays a heavy paw on the jackal's chest,
almost motherly. His mate
backs off a few yards. Eyeball
to eyeball, they face each other
before she bites into his belly
& tugs out the ropy entrails
like loops of wet gauze.
Time stops. She'd moved
through the tall yellow sage
as they copulated,
stood only a few feet
away, enveloped in the scent
that drew them together.
When they first saw her
there, they couldn't stop.
Is this how panic & cunning
seethe into the bloodstream?
Without the power to forgive,
locked in ritual, the fight
began before they uncoupled.
A vulture, out of the frame,
draws an unbroken spiral
against the plains & sky.
Black quills scribble
slow as the swing of a hypnotist's
gold chain. For a moment, it seems
she's snuggling up to the jackal.
Maybe the wild aroma of sex
plagues the yellow grass.
A drizzle adds its music
to the background,
& a chorus of young girls
chants from across the hills.
For a man who stumbles

on this scene, with Hegel
& awe in his head, he can't
say if his mouth is opened
by the same cry & song.

TROPIC OF CAPRICORN

THE TALLY

They're counting nails,
barrels of salt pork,
sacks of tea & sugar,
links of hemp, bolts of cloth
with dead colors, the whole
shape & slack of windy sails
down to galley planks
& clapboard hued by shame.
They're raising & lowering
an anchor clustered with urchins,
wondering if sandstone
can be taught a lesson
if inscribed with names & proclamations.
Snuff, powdered wigs—
redcoats run hands over
porcelain & silverware.
They're uncrating hymnals,
lace, volumes of Hobbes,
Rousseau, & kegs of rum.
Rats scurry across the deck
down the wharf, & a gaggle
of guinea fowl calls to lost sky
from a row of slatted boxes.
Knives & forks, wooden pegs,
balls of twine, vats of tallow,
& whet stones. They're counting women
& men: twenty-two prostitutes, ten
pickpockets, one forger, countless
thieves of duck eggs & black bread.
A soldier pries open a man's fists
to tally twelve marigold seeds—
here for lobbing off a half pound
of butter. Deck hands winch in
the drag of lines. A young officer
surveys the prettiest women, before
stashing *The Collected Quotations
of Pythagoras* for the governor.
Albatross perched on the mast

await another burial at sea,
shadowing a stoic nightingale
in a bamboo cage mended with yarn
where a red-headed woman kneels,
whispering his song to him.

HEROES OF WATERLOO

Here's the pub they conked
drunks over the head & shanghaied
them on carts rolled down shafts
to the quay. After schooners
of cider, I see the half-dazed
waking to sea monsters
outside The Heads.

Your hands anchor me to the antipodes
as "Stormy Monday Blues"
drowns the mermaid's lament,
& suddenly a man wants to bop
me over the head. The night
steals memories from sandstone
walls the convicts cut.

Larrikins shout middies of Strongbow
& point to the trapdoor
where Captain Hook hides
on the other side of jetlag.
But with your fingertips
at the nape, the blood's sextant,
I can't move beyond the body's true north.

WOKANMAGULLI

I searched all morning
for them along George Street,
paced The Rocks, corridors
of an invisible cellblock,
but only their absence
made them known. Later,
the surf of Botany Bay
licked out cups of sandstone.
In the Royal Botanic Gardens
I curled up in a cave
as if it waited one thousand
years for me. I weighed my body
against phantoms as car horns
shattered the afternoon.
Trees & flowers had eyes
like stones buried in a riverbed.

Why wasn't I happy
at parties where silhouettes
believed my fingers were jazz
riffs? Couldn't I have been
calm as dragonhead
under shaded glass
at the herbarium?
But when I felt the hearts
of bushrangers beat under
a plot of six shades of grass
like seeds of locoweed left
in the soil by the First Fleet,
it hurt not to speak.

Gnarled figs & ghost gums
slouched into a corroboree
of ring-barked old men.
My grandfather stood before me.
A nude peered from a fire
of waterlilies, but I had to look
through his eyes to see her

smile chiseled in Greek
marble. I tore off
their metal tags,
& my tongue weighed more
than I could balance
as I renamed them
for dead loved ones.

WARATAH

Love & pain converge
     to the point of a yellow
   pencil pressed against paper.

At the angle you sit
     the Centrepoint Tower
   is a gigantic lampshade

retrieving your face
     from that old world
   breaking through oils.

Something disturbs the calm
     like a hand through water,
   unromantic as a corpse

hugging a bloated sack
     of poisoned flour slumped
   beside a billabong.

That green in the sky
     isn't there till dark
   eases across the canvas.

It isn't the Beaujolais
     stealing thoughts on death
   & slamming twilight up

against the buildings.
     The Medusa tongues
   on the kitchen table

pull us into a frame
     to create tension
   that keeps them alive.

NEW GOLD MOUNTAIN

Families & dreams chained
to merchants back in Hong Kong,
men drifted to Hsin Chin Shan.

Sails clouded Guichen Bay
quick as brush strokes
against an unreal sky,
vipers in a field of skeletons.

They worked tailings in stamp mills
at Bendigo & Rocky River
before their stores & joss houses

burned down to a pouch of dust.
Blue distance & green mystery
of *Chinatown in Creswick*
highlighted by burnt orange.

Cobb & Co stagecoached horses
into anthills, trying to outrun
the vigilante's dustdevils

whose anger & indigo ignited
kerosene lanterns at Burrangong.
They clawed the earth to get
to suns inside rock, proving

the good in some men
can only half fill
a gold thimble.

WHITE LADY

Something to kill songs
& burn the guts, to ride
& break the hippocampus.
Something to subdue
the green freedom of crows
at Slaughterhouse Creek.
Milk mixed with gin or metho—
something to finish the job
guns & smallpox blankets
didn't do, to prod women
& seduce gods to dance
among trees, letting silver bark
uncurl into an undressed season.
Something to undermine those who
refuse to dangle brass breastplates
from their necks like King Billy.

Something to erase the willy wagtail
from vesperal leaves. No one
can sniff the air & walk miles
straight to water anymore.
Their heads fill with wings
& then they touch down again
like poisoned butterflies
bumping into bougainvillea.
Fringe dwellers languish,
piles of old clothes under gums.
White Lady is their giddy queen,
her arms flung around sleeping
children, ruling dreams
with an iron scepter,
her eyes screwed into them
like knots in bloodwood.

MEDITATIONS ON A DINGO

The smell of ubiquitous
blood on grass rekindles
the morning she chewed off
her leg. Sniffing left
& right, she plunges into a ravine.
If this is a man's totem,
he must cross the river
of amnesia. In a labyrinth
of familiar scents, nosing
her way around milk thistle,
she eyes her three-footed tracks
printed like stars in clay.
Another ewe has been herded
into the corner of a fence,
& repose wounds the sky.

Can she take a stone in her mouth
& drop it to spring a trap,
before eating the bait
under a pregnant moon? Sunrise
creeps over sandstone. Before
the fever breaks, you're on a hill
cradling a Winchester.
She's there, a few feet
from the rock you're standing
on. You think about the woman
you haven't touched for weeks,
before calling out to Beatrice.
Abetted by a mirage, as you
squeeze the trigger, a shadow
shakes blossoms from a bush.

No, please! Then night
scabs over. Is it a call
for help, or a magpie
drugged with starlight?
They goaded him in drunk,
leaning against his totem.
But now he trembles
& pisses on the cell floor,
as cries echo over grasstrees
& wind down to Cat Camp Creek,
Garibaldi Rock—meeting other cries
from South Florida, Transvaal,
Santiago, etching a blue map.
What they want him to sing
can't fit into his mouth.
Green tree frogs & stars are
good listeners, spreading out
till human dust grows into one
compendious anthem. *No,
please!* resounds. Bear hugs
& hammerlocks tilt the world
inside his head. But he won't
climb into a noose, won't lift
himself like a swan diver
off The Gap. That same
Cyclops stares through
the bars, a Tasmanian tiger
telling what his silence means
to the cricket in tussock.

IN THE MIRROR

Joey, you're behind shades
borrowed from Teach on page 67
of *The Australian Woman's Mirror*
March 29, 1961. Under the canopy

of a wide hat, with notebook & pencil,
you gaze out across the Kimberleys,
one step from the corner of time
crawling from a rainbow serpent's cave.

Less than the Crown of Thorns
along the Great Barrier Reef,
I look to see if a crack's started
in the black porcelain of your face.

No, I haven't swum the Fitzroy
near the Liveringa Sheep Station
or felt as small as you, Joey,
under the bigness of your sky,

but I hope you've outlasted
pages I found in the Opportunity Shop
where silver moths began years ago
to eat away your name.

THE PICCOLO

"There's Ayisha,"
you say, pointing to a wall
yellowing with snapshots
& theatre posters. Her face
wakes Piaf & Lady Day
on the jukebox, swelling this
12 x 12 room. A voice
behind the espresso machine
says Ayisha's in town,
& another says No,
she's back in New York.
Everyone's like Ehrich
Weiss in a tiger cage,
a season to break
things & make ourselves
whole. Someone puffs a J
rolled in perfumed paper,
& in my head I'm scribbling
you a love note, each word
sealed in amber. A cry
seethes from a semi-dark
corner, hidden like potato
eyes in a root cellar. My lips
brush your right cheek.
It's St. Valentine's Day,
but there's no tommy gun
in a violin case from Chicago
because it is your birthday.
You buy another sweet
for me, & when I take a bite
I taste desire. Another
dollar's dropped into the box:
Bud Powell's "Jor-Du"
fills The Piccolo,
& we move from one truth
to the next. Fingers
on the keys, on the spine.
Passion & tempo. We kiss

& form the apex that knows
what flesh is, the only
knot made stronger
by time & pressure.

JOHN SAYS

I'm more medicine
      than man. His hair
a white roar on the corner
      of Roslyn & Darlinghurst.
I'm thinking yellow
      skirts grow shorter
when streets are sad.
      On tonight's furlough
from the psychiatric ward,
      he throws his baseball cap
to the sidewalk & recites
      "Kubla Khan". Working
the crowd closer, he segues
      into "Snowy River" &
"Marriage" in Lear's voice.
      After years of Thorazine,
Hamlet & Caliban still
      share his tongue. Coins
rain into his upturned cap,
      & the crowd drifts toward
The Love Machine
      & McDonald's, before
he scoops up the money
      & dashes to a milkbar
across the street. Sometimes
      among blossoms, we imprison
each other with what we know
      & don't say beneath the moon's
striptease. John's back
      sitting near the footpath.
Between sips of Coke,
      he talks about Strasberg
& his birth on Australia Day,
      as his pink artificial leg
glows like a nude doll.
      A week later at Rozelle,
we're on a red arched bridge
      Japanese POWs erected

in a garden of flame trees.
       He tells almost the same story
Harry told about the LSD
       one Friday night in April,
what God kept telling him.
       Harry said an axe was used,
but John says he cut off a leg
       with a power saw. The trees
ignite the brook. A smile
       flashes among the goldfish,
& he says, *This is what love made me do.*

CORNERS OF NIGHT

Their love for Mickey Mouse
& Sleeping Beauty, for blue
jeans & cosmic pinball
backdrops the black rain
of Little Boy & Fat Man.
Madame Butterfly's kimono
branches into cherry trees
as Japanese in *America's Cup*
T-shirts gaze into strip clubs
& Lebanese take-aways.
But no trick photography
can erase *White Australia*
till it's a subtitle for Kabuki
masks. Two young men from Osaka
fire flashbulbs at a blonde
posed beneath the Norgen-
Vaaz ice cream sign,
draped in a T-shirt mini.
She seems to know everything
about gods, how to reverse
Circe's curse. The men pay
five dollars a pose, as she
tucks each bill between her breasts,
saying, "I don't sleep
with the enemy." They smile
& bow. She slips a foot
in & out of a red shoe.
Silhouettes burn into stone
walls & earth. Three years
later, standing a block away
from the ice cream sign,
she goes back. Now,
with shadows washing out
as much of her face
night's mercy can undo,
they'll know how light

corrupts the body of an angel
who stands on a city corner
to make a street musician
play his sax three times harder.

MESSAGES

They brand themselves with hearts
& dragons, *omni vincit amor*
wreathing the handles of daggers,
skulls with flowers between teeth,
& dotted lines across throats
saying *c-u-t-a-l-o-n-g-h-e-r-e.*
Epigraphs chiseled into marble
glisten with sweat.
Madonna quivers on a bicep
as fingers dance over a pinball machine.
Women pose with x's drawn through names
to harden features & bring knifethrowers
into their lives. A stripper in the neon
doorway of The Pink Pussycat
shows how the tattoo artist's hands
shook, as if the rose
were traced on her skin
with carbon paper & colored-in by bad luck . . .
red as a lost cartographer's ink.
A signature under her left nipple.

VISITATION

Dad was saying they've duplicated us
for eons & can read minds,
& there are two elders
who know where their portraits
hide in a cave of red ochre,
that all we have to do is
watch the animals to know
if they desire to govern the air.
That's the year Lucy Macpherson
broke my heart, the moment I knew
my bargi, Gran, was dead. Outside
Cape Tribulation, I circled midnight
paths, afraid I'd disappear. Now,
this doesn't go back to Goodah
when he lost his sacred fire
in Oola-pikka's whirlwind
& the lyrebird spoke of gods.
Carried away by Lucy's big smile
& sway of her hips, my feet
couldn't touch earth.
I felt her eyes from an afternoon
thicket, & till then I never broke
a horse with so much ease.
Beneath the Southern Cross,
I saw a Girramay man hanging in gaol
by his belt. Dad removed the spell
when he gripped my shoulder,
telling about the sky gods
who took people aboard ships
& made x-ray drawings. The Seven
Sisters grew so young, I was there
chanting witchetty grubs from the soil.
A scrub-hen shook a fig tree at sunset
when I woke singing the Honey Ant's
love song. A flying fox's shadow ran me home.

BENNELONG'S BLUES

You're here again, old friend.
You strut around like a ragtag redcoat
bellhop, glance up for a shooting star
& its woe, & wander in & out the cove
you rendezvoused with Governor Phillip
after Wil-le-me-ring speared him beside a beached
whale. We've known each other for years.
You're unchanged. But me, old scapegoat,
I never knew I was so damn happy
when we first met. Each memory
returns like heartbreak's boomerang.
You didn't tell me you were a scout,
a bone pointer, a spy,
someone to stand between new faces
& gods. I didn't know your other four
ceremonial names, hero in clownish clothes,
till another dead man whispered into my ear.

QUATRAINS FOR ISHI

When they swoop on you hobbled there
almost naked, encircled by barking dogs
at daybreak beside a slaughterhouse
in Oroville, outside Paradise,

California, draped in a canvas scrap
matted with dung & grass seed,
slack-jawed men aim rifles
at your groin. *Wild Man*

hums through telegraph wires,
as women from miles around
try to tame your tongue
by cooking family recipes

& bringing bowls of ambrosia
to the jail. Hungry & sick,
lonely & scared, you never touch
the food. Not even the half-breeds

can open your mouth with Wintu,
Spanish, & Maidu. Days pass
till an anthropologist faces you
with his list of lost words,

rolling them off his tongue
like beads of old honey. But you
are elsewhere, covering your head
with a mourning cap of pine pitch,

in earshot of Wild Horse Corral,
as winds steal prayers of the dead
from Kingsley Cave. It takes
more than years of moonlight

to torch bones down to ashes
to store in a rock cairn
at Mill Creek. You are there,
Ishi, with the last five men

strong enough to bend bows,
with the last twelve voices
of your tribe. When you hear
the anthropologist say *siwini*,

the two of you dance
& bang your hands against
the wooden cot, running fingers
along the grain of yellow pine.

On Main Street, where gold
fever left the air years ago,
you're now The Wild Man of Oroville
beside a new friend. When the train

whistles, you step behind a cottonwood
shading the platform, afraid of The Demon
your mother forbade you to venture near.
What is it, does a voice call to you

out of windy chaparral,
out of Wowunupo mu tetna,
to urge you back? Down
that rainbow of metal light

& sparks—then ferried across
Carquinez Straits—to the Oakland Mole.
The Golden Gate frames water
meeting sky, as a trolley car

lumbers uphill to your new home
at the Museum of Anthropology.
Here, in this ancient dust
on artifacts pillaged from Egypt

& Peru, I know why a man like you
laughs with one hand over his mouth.
Also, I know if I think of you
as me, you'll disappear. Ishi,

you're like a Don Juan
sitting beside Mrs. Gifford
calling birds. Who's Miss Fannie
in this photo from St. Louis?

Friend, what can you say
about these stone charms
from Lone Pine & England,
& are you still going to Chico

for that *Fiesta Arborea?*
How about this Sierra Club
walk from Buena Vista Park?
Here's another sack of acorns,

a few bundles of buckeye, hazel
shoots & alder. There's a sadness
in these willow branches, but no mock
orange. Pine needles have taught me

humility, & I'll never string
a bow or chip a blade from a block
of obsidian. The salmon harpoon
glides through the air as if

your mind entered the toggles
& shaft. I walk backwards
into Bear's Hiding Place
like you showed me—coming when

gone, on the other side of the river
standing here beside you, a snare
of milkweed coiled on the ground
like a curse inside a dream.

Back in your world of leaves,
you journey ten thousand miles
in a circle, hunted for years
inside the heart, till you wake

talking to a shadow in a robe
of wildcat pelts. Here
the day's bright as the purse
you carry your sacred tobacco in.

Your lungs are like thumbprints
on a negative, with you at a hospital
window as workmen walk girders:
All a same monkey-tee. I know why

a man doesn't sleep with the moon
in his face, how butter steals
the singing voice, & how a frog
cures a snakebite. At the museum

in your counting room, we gaze
down at the divided garden, past
beaded phantoms on streetcorners
perfumed with incense & herbs,

signalling the hills closer
where eucalyptus stores up oils
for a new inferno in the Sutro
Forest. Here's your five hundred

& twenty half dollars
saved in thirteen film cases—
your unwound watch now ticks
as the pot of glue hardens

among your arrows & knots
of deer sinews. March 25
at noon is as good a time to die
as to be born. A bluish sun

conspires to ignite the pyre
of bone awls & pendants of Olivella
shells, as a bear stands in Deer Creek
waving a salmon at the sky.

—for Luzma

THE GLASS ARK

(Two paleontologists working inside a glassed-in cubicle at La Brea Tar Pits)

M: How could you hear him
       When we were making love?

W: Voices rise.

M: Over love making?

W: Last week, you said
       You loved how birdsongs
       Drifted into the bedroom.

M: I didn't hear anything.

W: I heard him say, Please
       Don't. Don't hurt me,
       Martin.

M: I didn't hear anything
       But your love moans.

W: I'm going to tell
       What I heard.
       Every sigh.
       Every plea.
       Everything.

M: Where would I be?

W: Are you worried about
       Your Miss Whatshername?

M: We hear things.
       We see things.
       We make the clavicle
       Into an angel.

W: A window's bottom sash
    Swells with memories.

M: Sometimes you can read salvation
    Beneath sage brush & cypress,
    But wonder how anyone
    Ever dreamt these bones
    Were their livestock
    That wandered off a blind path.

W: Maybe if I were La Brea Woman,
    Nothing but a carbon-dated skull
    You can hold like a crystal ball
    & ask unfathomable questions,
    You'd count each seashell
    On my necklace a thousand times.

M: I heard a mourning dove
    Caught there, singing
    From a place
    Deep as regret's
    Tar pit.

W: Can they read
    The lies
    On our lips
    Through glass?

M: They stroll in,
    Thinking of Noah's Ark,
    But leave here knowing
    This is no place
    To come & argue with God.

W: We bury things
    Like dogs bury bones,
    & sneak back under moonglow
    To boxes of dirt & absence.

M: I used to have nightmares
    When I first started here.

Too many animal shadows
In limbo, stopped
On the edge.

W: Waiting for the *Cathartes aura,*
     For a turkey vulture
     To tangle his beak
     In death.
     How can you listen to bones
     Speak to ice flowers,
     & not hear his voice
     Begging for help last night?

M: We were making love,
     As Chet Baker's horn
     Filled the bedroom.

W: You can't stop me
     From hearing him.

M: We could always make love
     Right here beneath this
     Row of high-intensity lights.
     Can you see our faces
     On the frontpage
     Of *The L.A. Times,*
     Is that your desire?

W: Why didn't we yell down,
     Why did we wait for sirens
     To crimson the windowpanes?

M: It was a night lie,
     Like a paper airplane pulled
     To a furnace of neon
     & avarice.

W: You have no backbone.

M: It isn't my backbone
    You're condemned to praise,
    Sweetheart.

W: I've been sleeping
    With a stranger for three months.

M: I heard nothing.

W: I want you . . .
    I want you to brave
    Daylight, to be
    Heroic as midnight,
    To pull me into your arms
    & make me feel
    I'm not insane.

M: You're not insane.

W: I see the dead man
    Kneeling in dust,
    While he begs Martin
    Not to kill him.

M: You're not insane.

W: Why didn't you stop.

M: I couldn't.

W: You wouldn't . . .
    Wouldn't let me up.

M: I couldn't.

W: Why are their faces pressed
    Against the glass?
    Are they reading lips?
    Why is there no privacy
    In this world?

M: I heard him say,
Please stop,
Martinez.

W: Do you hear kerosene
When I say Pleistocene?

M: He said *Martinez*.

W: Liar.

M: Martinez.

W: Do you hear *Equus occidentalis* if—
When I say Angel Margolis?

M: Please.

DEBRIEFING GHOSTS

NUDE INTERROGATION

Did you kill anyone over there? Angelica shifts her gaze from the Janis Joplin poster to the Jimi Hendrix, lifting the pale muslin blouse over her head. The blacklight deepens the blues when the needle drops into the first groove of "All Along the Watchtower." I don't want to look at the floor. *Did you kill anyone? Did you dig a hole, crawl inside, and wait for your target?* Her miniskirt drops into a rainbow at her feet. Sandalwood incense hangs a slow comet of perfume over the room. I shake my head. She unhooks her bra and flings it against a bookcase made of plywood and cinderblocks. *Did you use an M-16, a handgrenade, a bayonet, or your own two strong hands, both thumbs pressed against that little bird in the throat?* She stands with her left thumb hooked into the elastic of her sky-blue panties. When she flicks off the blacklight, snowy hills rush up to the windows. *Did you kill anyone over there? Are you right-handed or left-handed? Did you drop your gun afterwards? Did you kneel beside the corpse and turn it over?* She's nude against the falling snow. *Yes.* The record spins like a bull's-eye on the far wall of Xanadu. *Yes,* I say. *I was scared of the silence. The night was too big. And afterwards, I couldn't stop looking up at the sky.*

THE POPLARS

Half in Monet's colors, headlong into this light, like someone lost along Daedalus' footpath winding back into the brain, hardly here. Doubts swarm like birds around a scarecrow—straw pulled from underneath a work cap.

Church bells alloy the midwest sky. How many troubled feet walked this path smooth? Is it safe to go back to Chu Lai? She's brought me halfway home again, away from the head floating down into my out-stretched hands.

I step off the path, sinking into one-hundred-years of leaves. Like trapped deer, we face each other. Her hand in his. His blue eyes. Her Vietnamese face. Am I a ghost dreaming myself back to flesh?

I stand in the skin's prison. A bluejay squawks till its ragged song pulls me out into the day burning like a vaporous temple of joss sticks. June roses in beds of mulch and peat moss surround me. I hear her nervous laughter at my back, among the poplars.

I can't hear my footsteps. I stop, turn and gaze at the lovers against an insistent green like stained glass. I walk toward a car parked near the church. Birds sing and flit in the raucous light. I hear the car's automatic locks click, sliding like bullets into the chamber of a gun.

On Third Street, the morning's alive with coeds hurrying into the clangor of bells, Saturday night asleep beneath their skin. Flowers herd them toward Jesus—cutworms on the leaves, at the roots.

SURGERY

Every spring, sure as the dogwood's clockwork, someone hacksaws off Odysseus' penis. And it lies dumbly at his feet, a doorknocker to a limestone castle, the fountain straying out a Medusa halo. In this watery mist, with a contrary sunlight glinting the bronze, there's only an outline of Eumaeus handing a quiver of arrows and a bow to him. Rivulets of water make the penis tremble, as if it were the final, half-alive offering to the gods.

Fifty yards past the fountain, on the other side of the quad, I step among lotus-eaters sunning in each other's arms. Mockingbirds and jays squabble overhead, dive-bombing Dutch elms. This unholy racket doesn't phase sunbathers and tree surgeons. As if they're fathering their destruction, branches fall into a pile, and the workmen pack beetle-eaten crevices with a white medicine, something like mortar—whiter than flesh.

I stop beneath an elm and clutch a half-dead branch. Momentarily, there's an old silence thick as memory. Claymores pop. Rifles and mortars answer, and then that silence again, as the slow light of tripflares drifts like a thousand falling handkerchiefs, lighting the concertina woven with arms and legs of sappers. Flares tied to little parachutes like magnolia blooming in the wounded air.

The sunbathers retreat into their abodes and the workmen feed the last branches into a big orange machine. The fountain's drained, and a man kneels before Odysseus. He holds the penis in one hand and a soldering torch in the other, his face hidden behind a black hood, beading a silver seam perfect enough to mend anyone's dream.

PHANTASMAGORIA

The two prisoners slump like baskets of contraband rice, blue sky pushing past. The doorgunner rocks his M-60, drifts on a cloud, and the day's whole machine shakes like a junkie's hand.

"*Anh hieu?* You understand, VC? *Lai-dai, lai-dai!*"

When the sergeant drags papa-san to the chopper door, I see J.L. and Philly face-down in the rice paddie. Smoke curls like a dragon in the trees, and the wind's anger whips the old man like a flag for a phantom ship. "Can you fly motherfucker, you some kinda gook angel?"

He dances, holds on, knowing the boy will talk when he lets go.

*

He glides along air, on magic, on his Honda, shooting American officers with a .45. Saigon nights hide this Tiger Lady, eyes like stones on a river bottom. In his breezy *ao dai* he's a cheap thrill, gunning his motorcycle, headed for a tunnel in the back of his mind lit by nothing but blood, just a taillight outdistancing the echo.

*

We slept side by side in the sand-bagged bunker, with arms around each other, too scared to see black and white. We didn't know how deeply hearts took sides on foreign shores, that only the metallic whine of rockets broke down barriers.

We'd lay down a fire that melted machineguns, but back in The World we threw up fences laughter couldn't shake. The bridge we rigged with our bodies, did we know it would crumble into dust and light?

When we stepped off the plane, you kissed the ground and disappeared. I put on my time-woven mask. But wherever you are, please know I won't say I heard you cry out in your sleep those burning nights—like you didn't hear me.

*

In the Ville Cholon, you can buy photos of your sister in bed with the yardman back in Muskogee. Spanish fly, counterfeiting plates of $20 bills, mother-of-pearl stash boxes, 9mm tie-clasp pistols, stilettos, M-16s packed in Cosmoline, French ticklers, snakeskin belts and boots, girlie magazines, German hand grenades, pieces of cardboard you scratch to sniff the perfume of round-eyed women, pirated editions of *War and Peace* and Genet's *Les Negres*, tapes by The Mothers of Invention, baseball cards, Mickey Mouse watches, and bubblegum machines rigged to explode months later. Subscriptions for Ten Easy Lessons in Writing Successful Love Letters in three colors of disappearing ink, chromeplated AK-47s, Alicante knives playing with sunlight, silver coke spoons and needles, a French perfume called Loneliness in a Bright Bottle, subway maps of New York City, secret diagrams of The Kremlin and Pentagon in Day-Glo, mink-lined gloves, cartons of Zippos, and snapshots of your dead buddies in Kodak living color.

*

Bikinied women tattooed with 900 numbers dance between third downs and beer ads. They take him back to an afternoon at L.A. International Airport as he gazes at his hands, fascinated by the moons on his fingernails.

He looks up. She uncrosses her legs. Her miniskirt opens like a pearl fan, a blur of shuffled cards. He could fly to Peoria, or go to The Big Apple to see the Statue of Liberty. Maybe she's looking past him, beyond the day's swift colors of tropical fish.

She's shampooing his hair, letting her fingers trail down his torso. A cloud of lather engulfs him. He feels the jungle's sweat and dirt let go, and memories whirl down the drain. Her touch drives blood to his fingertips, his scalp, his cock.

Another fumble and a replay. Another beer ad. More 900 numbers—look-alikes of Susie Wong and Eartha Kitt writhe on a red sofa. First and ten on the twenty-yard line. Halfback around the left flank, and another yard gained.

The soap burns his eyes. The room dances. An animal sound runs through him when he hears the motel door slam shut. He stumbles over to the nightstand and holds up her forty dollars, but his wallet and AWOL bag are gone. He stands there half-soaped, calling every woman's name he's ever known.

The kick's good. Cheerleaders cartwheel and toss batons into the air. Their glittered bodies turn into strobes and the afternoon becomes a chessboard. He's lost another fifty bucks on the Wildcats.

She'll discover the snapshots of his girlfriends, Eloise and Mary, back in Peoria. The nude of the fifteen-year-old he stayed with a week in Hong Kong. A pack of rubbers sealed in milky oil. The lock of his mother's hair that kept him alive in Danang. She'll find socks and underwear, shaving cream and a razor, and a handkerchief monogrammed with his dead grandfather's initials.

Three minutes left in the game. He's thinking, All the Wildcats need is an interception. No more timeouts left. He has seen miracles happen before. From his highschool days, he can feel in his body that they are about to run the wishbone.

Maybe she'll hang the Pentax around her neck. But as she peers closer, inside the AWOL bag's right pocket, she'll find what looks like two apricot halves. As he pictures her lifting them to her face, her red lips only inches away, he smiles. She won't know the scent, but she'll hear all the phantom voices of the rice paddie.

*

He leaves his Purple Heart under her negligee in a dresser drawer, and hitchhikes the mesa's burning rim. His footsteps blur the living and the dead, as faces float up from the jungle, each breath unstitching the landscape. He counts telephone poles to fall asleep in Blanco, conjuring-up a woman in Bac Ha.

No, it wasn't easy to let his girlfriend and Jody walk into that motel back in Phoenix. Why hadn't he been as merciful with the boy beside the ammo cache when he stepped into daylight? For weeks he walks around with his hands shoved deep into his pockets, gazing up at the Rockies, till feeling steals back to his fingers.

*

Girl, we were out celebrating Willie's promotion at The Plant. Candle-light, champagne, roses, a hundred-dollar dinner at The Palace. You won't believe how fast it came over him. In a finger snap. A cornered look grew on his face when a Vietnamese waitress walked over to our table. First, I thought he was making eyes at her. You know how Willie is. She was awful pretty. But with no warning he started to shout. The man raised hell for an hour, talking about ground glass in the food. He didn't even know who I was. Girl, it took three cops with a straitjacket to carry him away.

A SUMMER NIGHT IN HANOI

When the moviehouse lights click off and images flicker-dance against the white walls, I hear Billie's whispered lament. *Ho Chi Minh: The Man* rolls across the skin of five lynched black men, branding them with ideographic characters.

This scene printed on his eyelids is the one I was born with. My face is up there among the poplar leaves veined into stained glass. I'm not myself here, craving a mask of silk elusive as his four aliases.

He retouches photographs, paints antiques, gardens, cooks pastries, and loves and hates everything French. On his way to Chung-king to talk with Chiang K'ai-shek about fighting the Japanese, as day runs into night, he's arrested and jailed for fourteen months. Sitting here in the prison of my skin, I feel his words grow through my fingertips till I see his southern skies and old friends where mountains are clouds. As he tosses kernels of corn to carp, they mouth silent O's through the water.

Each face hangs like swollen breadfruit, clinging to jade leaves. How many eyes are on me, clustered in the hum of this dark theatre? The film flashes like heat lightning across a southern night, and the bloated orbs break open. Golden carp collage the five faces. The earth swings on a bellrope, limp as a body bag tied to a limb, and the moon overflows with blood.

A REED BOAT

The boat's tarred and shellacked to a water-repellent finish, just sway-dancing with the current's ebb, light as a woman in love. It pushes off again, cutting through lotus blossoms, sediment, guilt, unforgivable darkness. Anything with half a root or heart could grow in this lagoon.

There's a pull against what's hidden from day, all that hurts. At dawn the gatherer's shadow backstrokes across water, an instrument tuned for gods and monsters in the murky kingdom below. Blossoms lean into his fast hands, as if snapping themselves in half, giving in to some law.

Slow, rhetorical light cuts between night and day, like nude bathers embracing. The boat nudges deeper, with the ease of silverfish. I know by his fluid movements, there isn't the shadow of a bomber on the water anymore, gliding like a dream of death. Mystery grows out of the decay of dead things—each blossom a kiss from the unknown.

When I stand on the steps of Hanoi's West Lake Guest House, feeling that I am watched as I gaze at the boatman, it's hard to act like we're the only two left in the world. He balances on his boat of Ra, turning left and right, reaching through and beyond, as if the day is a woman he can pull into his arms.

THE HANOI MARKET

It smells of sea and earth, of things dying and newly born. Duck eggs, pig feet, mandarin oranges. Wooden bins and metal boxes of nails, screws, ratchets, balled copper wire, brass fittings, jet and helicopter gadgets, lug wrenches, bolts of silk, see-through paper, bamboo calligraphy pens, and curios hammered out of artillery shells.

Faces painted on coconuts. Polished to a knife-edge or sealed in layers of dust and grease, cogs and flywheels await secret missions. Aphrodisiacs for dream merchants. A silent storm moves through this place. Someone's worked sweat into the sweet loaves of bread lined up like coffins on a stone slab.

She tosses her blonde hair back and smiles down at everyone. Is it the squid and shrimp we ate at lunch, am I seeing things? An adjacent stall blooms with peacock feathers. The T-shirt wavers like a pennant as a sluggish fan slices the humidity,

I remember her white dress billowing up in a blast of warm air from a steel grate in New York City, reminding me of Miss Firecracker flapping like a flag from an APC antenna. Did we kill each other for this?

I stop at a table of figurines. What was meant to tear off a leg or arm twenty years ago, now is a child's toy I can't stop touching.

Maybe Marilyn thought she'd erase herself from our minds, but she's here when the fan flutters the T-shirt silkscreened with her face. The artist used five shades of red to get her smile right.

A door left ajar by a wedge of sunlight. Below the T-shirt, at the end of two rows of wooden bins, a chicken is tied directly across from a caged snake. Bright skin—deadly bite. I move from the chicken to the snake, caught in their hypnotic plea.

BURIED LIGHT

A farmer sings about the Fourth Moon, as a girl and boy push rice shoots under slush, their hands jabbing like quick bills of long-legged birds. Their black silk clothes shine in watery light.

Afternoon crouches like three tigers, the sun a disc against a dream of something better. The water buffalo walks with bowed head, as if there's a child beneath his hide, no longer a mere creature willed to the plow.

Mud rises, arcing across the sun. Some monolithic god has fallen to his knees. Dead stars shower down. It was there waiting more than twenty years, some demonic egg speared by the plowshare. Mangled legs and arms dance in the muddy water till a silence rolls over the paddie like a mountain of white gauze.

SHRINES

A few nightbirds scissor dusk into silhouettes . . . distant voices harmonize silences. Thatched houses squat against darkness, and the squares of light grow through doorways like boxes inside boxes. They've driven ancestors deeper into the jungles, away from offerings of rice and children's laughter. There's no serpent to guard these new shrines. The cameraman has tried to make an amputee whole again, as if he can see through a lover's eyes. Everything's paralyzed at twilight, except the ghostly jitterbug-flicker of videos from Hong Kong, Thailand, and America, with spellbound faces in Hanoi, Haiphong, Quang Tri, wherever electricity goes. The abyss is under the index finger on the remote control. As if losing the gift of speech, they fall asleep inside someone else's dream.

FRONTISPIECE

Walden Pond's crowded this Saturday afternoon, cars backed up to the main highway. There's an air show overhead. The Blue Angels zoom and zigzag prankish patterns across the flyway.

With a sharp U-turn, we're heading to where the Redcoats first fell in Concord. I can already see rows of stone the militia hid behind, like teeth grinning up from the ground.

A blond boy poses with a minuteman in a triangular hat. His father aims the camera. Can the three Vietnamese visitors see how our black hair makes the boy cower from something he reads in the father's face? The minuteman is dressed in garb the color of low hills. Before he retells the battle here, he says he received two Silver Stars in Danang. The Vietnamese take turns wearing the minuteman's hat and aiming his musket. A thread of smoke ties trees to sky, and when The Blue Angels break the sound barrier we duck and cover our heads with our hands.

At the souvenir shop, I buy *The Negro in the American Revolution* and give it to Thieu. His eyes dart from the book's frontispiece to my face: Jordan Freeman's killing Major William Montgomery at the Battle of Groton Heights. Huu Thinh studies the image also, and says that the American poets he likes best are Langston Hughes and Whitman.

Le Minh walks out into a tussle of tall grass surrounding a wooden bridge, and we follow her striped sun hat. Her high heels sink into the sandy soil that's held together by so many tiny, white roots. Burrs cling to her nylons. Now, it isn't hard to imagine her filling bomb craters along the Ho Chi Minh Trail or reading Jack London in some Laotian jungle. She's ahead of us. On a path that winds back like apparitions imprinted on the living, as if we need to quick-march through grass to prove we outfoxed time.

She climbs into the car, and begins to pick cockles off her stockings. We speed up like shadows overtaking men, smiling and huffing as if we've been making love an hour.

BREASTS

Our fingers played each other like a blue guitar, teaching the body how hands made the brain grow beyond the cave's light and fortress. You smelled of sassafras and Louisiana honeysuckle, but your breasts were two Moorish peaks on the edge of Xanadu. As a goldfish reflects the size of its glass bowl or weedy pond, that summer my hands grew to fit curves.

I still have a lumberjack or stevedore's hands. And Cousin, you remain silent as sin. Each embrace held blood's yoke. Kissed down to a blue feeling, we both fell for life and death. So many mouths, so many kisses, from twelve to the grave . . . the left breast, the right breast, a split between never again. But, no, I still can't believe God and Satan wrestle each other in every pound of flesh.

After your brother told me, I stood there and tried out the entire horoscope on my tongue, as if I needed to hold a stone in each hand to anchor myself under that red sky. Yes, I stood there like Judas, missing what I almost had—the bread and wine never tasted beneath the yellow trees. Still, I can't blame my hands for flying up to clutch a piece of heaven.

THE DECK

I have almost nailed my left thumb to the 2 x 4 brace that holds the deck together. This Saturday morning in June, I have sawed 2 x 6s, T-squared and levelled everything with three bubbles sealed in green glass, and now the sweat on my tongue tastes like what I am. I know I'm alone, using leverage to swing the long boards into place, but at times it seems as if there are two of us working side by side like old lovers guessing each other's moves.

This hammer is the only thing I own of yours, and it makes me feel I have carpentered for years. Even the crooked nails are going in straight. The handsaw glides through grease. The toenailed stubs hold. The deck has risen up around me, and now it's strong enough to support my weight, to not sway with this old, silly, wrong-footed dance I'm about to throw my whole body into.

Plumbed from sky to ground, this morning's work can take nearly anything! With so much uproar and punishment, footwork and euphoria, I'm almost happy this Saturday.

I walk back inside and here you are. Plain and simple as the sunlight on the tools outside. Daddy, if you'd come back a week ago, or day before yesterday, I would have been ready to sit down and have a long talk with you. There were things I wanted to say. So many questions I wanted to ask, but now they've been answered with as much salt and truth as we can expect from the living.

GHOST VIDEO

In the Golden Triangle Cafe, I see two waitresses tiptoe and reach for plates and teapots with scenes of Van Lang and Au Lac glazed in aquamarine. When they glide from behind the rice-paper screen angled between the kitchen and dining tables, their mouths peel open like poppies.

If I tilt my head to the left, there are three men in a side room. Two old faces play Mah-Jongg with two absent friends. They move to a song behind a closed door. Two defeated soldiers—three arms and three legs—dressed in jungle fatigues. There's no mercy or pride left in the faded cloth. Cigarette smoke curls up from each dark mouth, hanging like question marks. If they were in Cu Chi or Hue, they'd find words for the images in their heads. And the teenager beside them, what has he learned from these two as he sits hypnotized by a video? He's slumped in his chair, as if the last dream has been drained from him. The Mah-Jongg players bathe their hands in the video's wounded reflection. The boy has fallen in love with the actress, a ghost girl who walks through fortress walls.

The women stroll with teacups on their heads. The landmines never explode. Some days they brush each other with rice powder. After they've rehearsed beneath the kitchen's naked bulb, in a peppery mist of onion and garlic, they walk out into the world in miniskirts, with smiles stolen from the two concubines who knelt before Sun Tzu.

PHANTOM LIMBS

When you take her into your wounded embrace, a bra clasp unhooks itself. A leg, an arm—the piano in your mother's living room three blocks away still plays boogiewoogie when you shuffle in. After you returned, love slipped out a side door. But you knew the librarian with the bifocals, Miss Nancy, always had a crush on you. She sent you pecan cookies for a year, and you shared them with your squad till the point man hit a booby trap on the Ho Chi Minh Trail.

Your missing hand itches. You can hear your grandmother say, "I'm gonna get some money today." Your feet wander off together and leave you lost in soap operas and morphine. You're still strong enough not to wish you were someone else. You tell the guys at The Golden Day, "If that new waitress sits in my lap, I'll bet my other arm and leg she'll know I'm still one hundred per cent man."

Two dogs couple under a cottonwood, and Johnny four doors down throws stones at them. And there goes Mrs. Carson in her leopard-skin coat, talking to herself. A part of you waits in a brass urn on a windowsill. With women, this is a conversation-piece. As you sit there, balancing a plate on your knee, thinking about sprinkling the finest-ground pepper on your pizza, you gaze down at the avenue.

DREAM ANIMAL

He's here again. Is this hunger I smell, something like wildflowers and afterbirth tangled in sage? I press down on each eyelid to keep him here: otherwise, otherwise. . . . But he always escapes the lair. Don't care how much I dance and chant rain across the mountains, it never falls on his back. Tiger or wolf, he muzzles up to me, easy as a Christbird walking across lily pads. As if he slipped out of a time machine, his phantom prints disappear at the timberline. I'm on all fours, with my nose almost pressed to the ground. A few galah feathers decorate clumps of tussock. Ants have unlocked the mystery of a bearded dragon, as they inch him toward some secret door. I close my eyes again. Somewhere a kookaburra laughs. In this garden half-eaten by doubt and gunpowder, honeyeaters peck the living air. And here he stands beneath the Southern Cross, the last of his kind, his stripes even brighter in this dark, nocturnal weather.

TESTIMONY

I

He hopped boxcars to Chitown
late fall, just a few steps
ahead of the hawk. After
sleepwalking to the 65 Club,
he begged Goon for a chance
to sit in with a borrowed sax.
He'd paid his dues for years
blowing ravenous after-hours
till secrets filled with blues
rooted in Mississippi mud;
he confessed to Budd Johnson
that as a boy playing stickball,
sometimes he'd spy in a window
as they rehearsed back in K.C.

It was Goon who took him home,
gave him clothes & a clarinet.
Maybe that's when he first
played laughter & crying
at the same time. Nights
sucked the day's marrow
till the hibernating moon grew
fat with lies & chords. Weeks
later, with the horn hocked,
he was on a slow Greyhound
headed for the Big Apple,
& "Honeysuckle Rose"
blossomed into body language,
driven by a sunset on the Hudson.

II

Washing dishes at Jimmy's
Chicken Shack from midnight
to eight for nine bucks a week
just to hear Art Tatum's keys,
he simmered in jubilation
for over three months. After
a tango palace in Times Square
& jam sessions at Clark Monroe's,
in the back room of a chili house
on "Cherokee," he could finally play
everything inside his head,
the melodic line modulating
through his bones to align itself
with Venus & the Dog Star.

Some lodestone pulled him
to Banjo's show band on the highway
till Baltimore hexed him: a train
ticket & a telegram said a jealous
lover stabbed his father to death.
He followed a spectral cologne
till he was back with Hootie,
till that joke about chickens
hit by a car swelled into legend.
Now, he was ready to squeeze
elevenths, thirteenths,
every silent grace note
of blood into each dream
he dared to play.

III

Purple dress. Midnight-blue.
Dime-store floral print
blouse draped over a Botticellian
pose. Tangerine. He could blow
insinuation. A train whistle
in the distance, gun shot
through the ceiling, a wood warbler
back in the Ozarks at Lake
Taneycomo, he'd harmonize
them all. Celt dealing in coal
on the edge of swing. Blue
dress. Carmine. Yellow sapsucker,
bodacious "zoot suit with the reet
pleats" & shim sham shimmy.

Lime-green skirt. Black silk
petticoat. Velveteen masterpiece &
mindreader twirling like a spotlight
on the dance floor. Yardbird
could blow a woman's strut
across the room. "Alice in
Blue" & "The Lady in Red"
pushed moans through brass.
Mink-collared cashmere & pillbox.
Georgia peach. Pearlized facade
& foxtrot. Vermillion dress. High
heels clicking like a high hat.
Black-beaded flapper. Blue satin.
Yardbird, he'd blow pain & glitter.

IV

Moving eastward to the Deep
South with Jay McShann,
on trains whistling into dogwood
& pine, past shadows dragging balls
& chains, Bird landed in jail
in Jackson for lallygagging
on the front porch of a boardinghouse
with the lights on. For two days
he fingered a phantom alto
till "What Price Love" spoke
through metal & fluted bone.
The band roared through the
scent of mayhaw & muscadine,
back into Chicago & Detroit.

When the truckload of horns
& drums rolled into Manhattan,
Bird slid behind the wheel.
The three-car caravan
followed, looping Central Park
till a mounted policeman
brandished his handcuffs.
Days later, after moving into the Woodside,
after a battery of cutting contests,
Ben Webster heard them & ran downtown
to Fifty-second Street & said
they were kicking in the devil's door
& putting the night back
together up at the Savoy.

V

Maybe it was a day like today.
We sat in Washington Square Park
sipping wine from a Dixie cup
when Bird glimpsed Anatole
Broyard walking past & said,
"He's one of us, but he doesn't
want to admit he's one of us."
Maybe it was only guesswork
contorted into breath. We sat
staring after Anatole until he
disappeared down Waverly Place.
Bird took a sip, shook his head,
& said, "Now, that guy chases
heartbreak more than I do."

Maybe it was a day like today.
We were over at Max's house
as Bird talked Lenny
before Bruce was heard of,
telling a story about a club owner's
parrot squawking the magic word.
Maybe it was sunny or cloudy
with our tears, like other days
when Max's mama slid her key
into the front-door lock. Bird
would jump up, grab the Bible
& start thumbing through pages,
& Mrs. Roach would say, "Why
aren't you all more like Charlie?"

VI

If you favor your left
hand over the right, one
turns into Abel & the other
into Cain. Now, you
take Ikey, Charlie's half-brother
by an Italian woman, their father
would take him from friend
to friend, saying, "He's got good
hair." Is this why Charlie
would hide under his bed & play
dead till his mother kissed him
awake? No wonder he lived
like a floating rib
in a howl whispered through brass.

Always on the move, Charlie
traversed the heart's nine rings
from the Ozarks to le Boeuf
sur le Toit in Montmartre.
Though he never persuaded himself
to stay overseas, his first day
in Stockholm glowed among fallen
shadows. Always on some no-man's
land, he'd close his eyes
& fly to that cluster of Swedes
as he spoke of his favorite artist:
"Heifetz cried through his violin."
Charlie could be two places at once,
always arm-wrestling himself in the dark.

VII

Like a black cockatoo
clinging to a stormy branch
with its shiny head rocking
between paradise & hell,
that's how Yardbird
listened. He'd go inside
a song with enough irony
to break the devil's heart.
Listening with his whole body,
he'd enter the liquid machine
of cow bells & vibes,
of congas & timbales,
& when he'd raise his alto
a tropic sun beamed into the club.

Machito & his Afro-Cuban
Orchestra peppered the night
till Yardbird left ash in the bell
of his horn. He swore Africa
swelled up through the soles
of his feet, that a Latin beat
would start like the distant
knocking of tiny rods & pistons
till he found himself mamboing.
He must've known this is
the same feeling that drives
sap through mango leaves,
up into the fruit's sweet
flesh & stony pit.

VIII

He was naked,
wearing nothing but sky-
blue socks in the lobby
of the Civic Hotel in Little Tokyo,
begging for a quarter
to make a phonecall. The Chinese
manager led him back to his room,
but minutes later a whiff of smoke
trailed him down the staircase.
This was how six yellow pills
sobered him up for a recording
session. He was naked, & now
as firemen extinguished the bed
cops wrestled him into a straitjacket.

Camarillo's oceanic sky opened
over his head for sixteen months
when the judge's makeshift bench
rolled away from his cell door.
Eucalyptus trees guarded this
dreamtime. Yardbird loved
working his hands into the soil
till heads of lettuce grew round
& fat as the promises he made
to himself, lovers, & friends.
Saturday nights he'd blow
a C-melody sax so hard
he'd gaze into the eyes of the other patients
to face a naked mirror again.

IX

I can see him, a small boy
clutching a hairbrush.
This is 852 Freeman
Street, just after his father
took off on the Pullman line
with a porter's jacket
flapping like a white flag.
A few years later, he's astride
a palomino on Oliver Street
where a potbellied stove
glowed red-hot as a nightclub
down the block. Rudee Vallee
& late nights on Twelfth
haven't marked him yet.

When I think of Bird, bad
luck hasn't seethed into his body,
& Kansas City isn't Tom's
Town. This is before the silver
Conn bought on time, before Rebecca's
mother rented the second-floor,
before prophecies written on his back
at the Subway Club by Buster & Prez
on "Body & Soul," long before
Jo Jones threw those cymbals
at his feet, before benzedrine
capsules in rotgut & the needle's
first bite, before he was bittersweet
as April, when he was still Addie's boy.

X

My darling. My daughter's death
surprised me more than it did you.
Don't fulfill funeral proceeding until
I get there. I shall be the first
one to walk into our chapel.
Forgive me for not being there
with you while you are at
the hospital. Yours most sincerely,
your husband, Charlie Parker.
Now, don't say you can't hear
Bird crying inside these words
from L.A. to New York,
trying to ease Chan's pain,
trying to save himself.

My daughter is dead.
I will be there as quick
as I can. My name is Bird.
It is very nice to be out here.
I am coming in right away.
Take it easy. Let me be the first
one to approach you. I am
your husband. Sincerely,
Charlie Parker. Now, don't
say we can't already hear
those telegraph keys playing Bartok
till the mockingbird loses its tongue,
already playing Pree's funeral song
from the City of Angels.

XI

I believe a bohemian girl
took me to Barrow Street
to one of those dress-up parties
where nobody's feet touched
the floor. I know it was months
after they barred Bird
from Birdland. Months
after he drank iodine,
trying to devour one hundred
black roses. Ted Joans
& Basheer also lived there,
sleeping three in a bed
to keep warm. A woman dusted
a powdered mask on Bird's face.

I remember he couldn't stop
talking about Dali & Beethoven,
couldn't stop counting up gigs
as if tallying losses: the Argyle . . .
Bar de Duc. . . the Bee Hive . . .
Chanticleer . . . Club de Lisa . . .
El Grotto Room . . . Greenleaf Gardens . . .
Hi De Ho . . . Jubilee Junction . . .
Le Club Downbeat . . . Lucille's Band Box . . .
The Open Door . . . St. Nick's . . . Storyville.
I remember some hepcat talking about
vaccinated bread, & then Bird began
cussing out someone inside his head
called Moose the Mooche. I remember.

XII

Bird was a pushover, a soft
touch for strings, for the low
& the high, for sonorous catgut
& the low-down plucked ecstasy
of garter belts. He loved
strings. A medley of nerve endings
ran through every earth color: sky
to loam, rainbow to backbone
strung like a harp & cello.
But he never wrung true blues
out of those strings, couldn't
weave the vibrato of syncopated
brass & ghosts
till some naked thing cried out.

Double-hearted instruments breathed
beneath light wood, but no real flesh
& blood moaned into that unbruised
surrender. Did he think Edgard
Varese & Stefan Wolpe could help
heal the track marks crisscrossing
veins that worked their way back
up the Nile & down the Tigris?
Stravinsky & Prokofiev. Bird
loved strings. Each loveknot
& chord stitched a dream to scar
tissue. But he knew if he plucked
the wrong one too hard, someday a nightmare
would break & fall into his hands.

XIII

They asked questions so hard
they tried to hook the heart
& yank it through the mouth.
I smiled. They shifted
their feet & stood there
with hats in hands, hurting
for headlines: *Baroness Pannonica* . . .
I told them how I met my husband
at Le Touquet airport, about decoding
for De Gaulle, about my coming-out ball.
I said I heard a thunderclap,
but they didn't want to hear
how Charlie died laughing
at jugglers on the Dorsey show.

The Stanhope buzzed with innuendo.
Yes, they had him with a needle
in his arm dead in my bathroom.
They loved to hear me say that
he was so sick he refused a shot
of gin. I told them his body
arrived at Bellevue five hours
later, tagged John Parker.
I told them how I wandered
around the Village in circles,
running into his old friends,
that a cry held down my tongue
till I found Chan, but they only
wanted us nude in bed together.

XIV

They wanted to hold his Selmer,
to put lips to the mouthpiece,
to have their pictures snapped
beneath *Bird Lives! Bird Lives!*
scrawled across Village walls
& subway trains. Three women
sang over his body, but no one read
The Rubaiyat of Omar Khayyam
aloud. Two swore he never said
"Please don't let them bury me
in Kansas City." Everyone
has a Bird story. Someone
said he wished for the words
Bird recited for midnight fixes.

Someone spoke about a letter
in *Down Beat* from a G.I.
in Korea who stole back
a recording of "Bird in Paradise"
from a dead Chinese soldier's hand.
Someone counted the letters in his name
& broke the bagman's bank. Maybe
there's something to all this
talk about seeing a graven image
of Bird in Buddha & the Sphinx.
Although half of the root's gone,
heavy with phantom limbs, French
flowers engraved into his horn
bloom into the after-hours.

THE BLUE HOUR

BLESSING THE ANIMALS

Two by two, past
the portals of paradise,
camels & pythons parade.
As if on best behavior,
civil as robed billy goats
& Big Bird, they stroll
down aisles of polished stone
at the Feast of St. Francis.
An elephant daydreams, nudging
ancestral bones down a rocky path,
but won't venture near the boy
with a white mouse peeking
from his coat pocket. Beyond
monkeyshine, their bellows
& cries are like prayers
to unknown planets & zodiac
signs. The ferret & mongoose
on leashes, move as if they know
things with a sixth sense.
Priests twirl hoops of myrrh.
An Australian blue cattle dog
paces a heaven of memories—
a butterfly on a horse's ear
bright as a poppy outside
Urbino. As if crouched
between good & bad, St. John
the Divine grows in quintessence
& limestone, & a hoorah of Miltonic
light falls upon alley rats
awaiting nighttime. Brother
ass, brother sparrowhawk,
& brother dragon. Two
by two, washed & brushed down
by love & human pride,
these beasts of burden
know they're the first
scapegoats. After sacred

oils & holy water, we huddle
this side of their knowing
glances, & they pass through
our lives, still loyal to thorns.

RHYTHM METHOD

If you were sealed inside a box
within a box deep in a forest,
with no birdsongs, no crickets
rubbing legs together, no leaves
letting go of mottled branches,
you'd still hear the rhythm
of your heart. A red tide
of beached fish oscillates in sand,
copulating beneath a full moon,
& we can call this the first
rhythm because sex is what
nudged the tongue awake
& taught the hand to hit
drums & embrace reed flutes
before they were worked
from wood & myth. Up
& down, in & out, the piston
drives a dream home. Water
drips till it sculpts a cup
into a slab of stone.
At first, no bigger
than a thimble, it holds
joy, but grows to measure
the rhythm of loneliness
that melts sugar in tea.
There's a season for snakes
to shed rainbows on the grass,
for locust to chant out of the dunghill.
Oh yes, oh yes, oh yes, oh yes
is a confirmation the skin
sings to hands. The Mantra
of spring rain opens the rose
& spider lily into shadow,
& someone plays the bones
till they rise & live
again. We know the whole weight
depends on small silences
we fit ourselves into.

High heels at daybreak
is the saddest refrain.
If you can see blues
in the ocean, light & dark,
can feel worms ease through
a subterranean path
beneath each footstep,
Baby, you got rhythm.

THE PARROT ASYLUM

His vest of fifty pockets
woven from black nylon mesh
nestles against his skin,
snug as a WW II moneybelt.
His head is still up
in a tall eucalyptus,
gazing out over Kakadu
National Park. His body
throbs as if one hundred eyes
press against his ribcage—
a milkmaid's brood
between warm breasts.
He tries to daydream himself
into The Master Egg Thief
headline again, in a new Lexus
with a Madonna look-alike
speeding down a Dallas freeway.

It'll take years, maybe
two or three girlfriends
later, for him to arrive here
& linger like Pisthetairos
before this dome-shaped aviary
matted with red-tailed
cockatoo feathers. Once,
this one called Lily
knew more words than a child:
bloody . . . fool . . . our song . . .
Flicking raven hair
out of her eyes, Dr. Charcot,
the bird psychologist, says
that Parker's "Ornithology"
used to make them chatter
human voices. But now
they only gaze at the floor
or slant their heads sideways,
pecking the last fluff

from their pale bodies,
never facing the sun,
never speaking to the jester's
godlike shadow on the wall.

THE THORN MERCHANT'S DAUGHTER

When she cocks her head
the last carrier pigeon's ghost
cries out across a cobalt sky.
The glossy snapshot of her
draped in a sun-blanched dress
before a garden of stone phalluses
slants crooked in its gold frame.
She looks as if she's tiptoed
out of *Innocence Choosing Love
over Wealth*. A Janus-headed
figure tarries at a junction
with twelve versions of hell
& heaven. She's transfixed
by bluejays pecking dewy figs
down to the meaty promise of a heart.
She's *Mary Magdalen in the Grotto,*
& was eyeing Lee Morgan at Slugs'
when the pistol flash burned
through his solo. Her aliases
narrate tales from Nepal & Paris,
Texas, from Bathsheba to the woman
flaming like poppies against sky
at the theatre with John
Dillinger. To see her
straight, there's no choice
but to walk with a limp.

THE MONKEY HOUSE

He pressed his face against the bars,
watching the biggest male macaque
mount a statuesque female.
She gazed at the cage floor
& he looked up past
rafters of leaves & fiberglass,
squinting toward a sundial.
They were rocking back & forth,
grunting a chorus of muffled laughs.
A father covered his daughter's eyes
with both hands, but let his two sons look.
An old woman kept tugging
her husband's sleeve
as he stood munching Cracker
Jacks, searching for the toy
pistol or spinning top
at the bottom of the box.
He watched, stroking his beard,
a hundred yards away from the crowd
eating noontime sandwiches & sipping
thermoses of coffee. Joggers worked
the air with arms & legs,
& it seemed to him the monkeys
were making love to the rhythms
of the city. Also, he still can't
say why, but he was running
the term *ethnic cleansing* over
& over in his mind, like a stone
polishing itself in a box of sand.
There were tears in his eyes,
& he felt like he'd returned
to the scene of a crime.
When their bodies began to tremble
down to a split second, the other
monkeys began to slap the male
& beat his head like a drum.
Then, lost among the absurd
clocks, he turned to watch
leaves as they began to fall.

DOLPHY'S AVIARY

We watched Baghdad's skyline
ignite, arms & legs entwined
as white phosphorus washed over
our bedroom, the sounds of war
turned down to a sigh. It was one
of those nights we couldn't let go
of each other, a midwestern storm
pressing panes till they trembled
in their sashes. Eric Dolphy
scored the firmament splitting
to bedrock, as the wind spoke
tongues we tried to answer.
At first, we were inside
muted chords, inside an orgasm
of secrets, & then cried out,
"Are those birds?" Midnight
streetlights yellowed the snow—
a fleeing ghost battalion
cremated in the bony cages
of tanks in sand dunes. Dolphy said,
"Birds have notes between our notes . . ."
I could see them among oak rafters
& beams, beyond the burning cold,
melodious in cobweb & soot.
Like false angels up there
in a war of electrical wires
& bat skeletons caked with excrement,
we in winding sheets of desire
as their unbearable songs
startled us down.

CRACK

You're more jive than Pigmeat
       & Dolemite, caught by a high note
    stolen from an invisible saxophone.

I've seen your sequinned nights
       pushed to the ragged end
    of a drainpipe, swollen fat

with losses bitter as wormwood,
       dropped tongues of magnolia
    speaking a dead language.

You're an eyeload, heir
       to cotton fields & the North
    Star balancing on a needle.

Where's the loot, at Scarlett O'Hara's
       or buying guns for the Aryan Nation?
    The last time I saw you, fabulous

merchant of chaos, you were beating days
       into your image as South African
    diamonds sparkled in your teeth.

Cain's daughter waits with two minks
       in a tussle at her throat,
    fastened with a gold catch.

You pull her closer, grinning up
       at barred windows, slinky
    as a cheetah on a leash.

You're the Don of Detroit,
       gazing down from your condo
    at the night arranged into a spasm

band, & groupies try to steady hands
          under an incantation of lights,
     nailed to a dollarsign & blonde wig.

Desire has eaten them from the
          inside: the guts gone, oaths
     lost to a dictum of dust

in a worm's dynasty. Hooded
          horsemen ride out of a Jungian
     dream, & know you by your mask.

I see ghosts of our ancestors
          clubbing you to the ground.
     Didn't you know you'd be gone,

condemned to run down a John
          Coltrane riff years from Hamlet,
     shaken out like a white sleeve?

Bullbats sew up the evening
          sky, but there's no one left
     to love you back to earth.

NO-GOOD BLUES

1

I try to hide in Proust,
Mallarme, & Camus,
but the no-good blues
come looking for me. Yeah,
come sliding in like good love
on a tongue of grease & sham,
built up from the ground.
I used to think a super-8 gearbox
did the job, that a five-hundred-dollar suit
would keep me out of Robert Johnson's
shoes. I rhyme Baudelaire
with Apollinaire, hurting
to get beyond crossroads & goofer
dust, outrunning a twelve-bar
pulsebeat. But I pick up
a hitchhiker outside Jackson.
Tasseled boots & skin-tight
jeans. You know the rest.

2

I spend winter days
with Monet, seduced
by his light. But the no-good
blues come looking for me.
It takes at least a year
to erase a scar
on a man's heart. I come home nights
drunk, the couple next door
to keep me company, their voices
undulating through my bedroom wall.
One evening I turn a corner
& step inside Bearden's *Uptown
Sunday Night Session.* Faces
Armstrong blew from his horn
still hanging around the Royal Gardens—all
in a few strokes, & she suddenly leans out of
a candy-apple green door & says,
"Are you from Tougaloo?"

3

At The Napoleon House
Beethoven's *Fifth* draws shadows
from the walls, & the no-good blues
come looking for me. She's here,
her left hand on my knee.
I notice a big sign
across the street that says
The Slave Exchange.
She scoots her chair closer.
I can't see betrayal
& arsenic in Napoleon's hair—
they wanted their dying emperor
under the Crescent City's
Double Scorpio. But nothing
can subdue these African voices
between the building's false floors,
this secret song from the soil
left hidden under my skin.

4

Working swing shift at McGraw-
Edison, I shoot screws
into cooler cabinets as if I were born
to do it. But the no-good blues come
looking for me. She's from Veracruz,
& never wears dead colors of the factory,
still in Frida Kahlo's world of monkeys.
She's a bird in the caged air.
The machines are bolted down
to the concrete floor,
everything moves with the same big
rhythm Mingus could get out of
a group. Humming the syncopation
of punch presses & conveyer belts,
work grows into our dance
when the foreman
hits the speed-up button
for a one-dollar bonus.

5

My hands are white
with chalk at The Emporium
in Colorado Springs, but the no-good
blues come looking for me. I miscue
when I look up & see sunlight
slanting through her dress
at the back door. That shot
costs me fifty bucks.
I let the stick glide along the V
of two fingers, knowing men who
wager their first born to conquer
snowy roller coasters & myths.
I look up, just when
the faith drains out of
my right hand. It isn't
a loose rack. But more like—
well, I know I'm in trouble
when she sinks her first ball.

6

I'm cornered at Birdland
like a two-headed man hexing
himself. But the no-good blues
come looking for me. A prayer
holds me in place,
balancing this sequinned
constellation. I've hopped boxcars
& thirteen state lines to where
she stands like Ma Rainey.
Gold tooth & satin. Rotgut
& God Almighty. Moonlight
wrestling a Texas-jack.
A meteor of desire burns
my last plea to ash. Blues
don't care how many tribulations
you lay at my feet, I'll go
with you if you promise
to bring me home to Mercy.

SANDHOG

They tango half the night
before he can believe she isn't
Eurydice. The bandonean
& violin cornet pull them into an embrace
in an Eden burdened with fruits
out of season. He wants to punch
walls or elbow the pug-nosed bouncer,
Quasimodo, whose eyes caress Angelina
as they ascend. He tells himself
he isn't afraid of anything
or anyone, that he lives to work
in the abyss where a small stone can kill
if nudged free by a steel-toed boot.

The yellow cage on a whiny cable drags
the sun down. Almost in each other's arms,
hardhats descend into the caisson
where the air's giddy, humming "Sentimental
Journey," in the fraternity of sons
who follow fathers down past
omens: *Never take love this deep
into the ground.* He can hear her
say, "I can't endure a one-night
stand," as she pulls away & grabs
her beaded purse. Accents echo
through this inverted Tower of Babel
till nirvana grows into the East Tunnel.
With Angelina in his head, *Fire
in the hole* means a starry night.

THE WALL

But you shall shine more bright in these contents
Than unswept stone, besmeared with sluttish time.
　　　　　　　　　　—William Shakespeare

Lovenotes, a bra, lipstick
kisses on a postcard, locks
of hair, a cerulean bouquet,
baseball gloves broken in
with sweat & red dirt,
a fifth of Beefeaters,
everything's carted away.
Before it's tagged & crated,
a finger crawls like a fat slug
down the list, keeping record
for the unborn. All the gunshots
across America coalesce here
where a mother sends letters
to her son. As time flowers
& denudes in its whorish work,
raindrops tap a drumroll
& names fade till the sun
draws them again out of granite nighttime.

A STORY

She says he was
telling a dirty joke
about Asian women
working in a sweatshop
in Orange County, sewing
Ku Klux Klan robes & hoods
for The Redneck Discount
somewhere in South Carolina,
as Mary Black sang "Bright
Blue Rose" on the jukebox,
when the whine of airbrakes
& raw squeal of Goodyear tires
signalled the rig's thunderous
crash through the Sundowner's
neon facade, that it's funny
how no one else was hurt
when the truck uprooted
the big redbud out front
& showered the whole day
with flowers & bone.

WHAT COUNTS

I thumb pages, thinking onion
or shreds of garlic
flicked into my eyes.
Maybe the light's old,
or the earth begs every drop
of water it dares to caress.
I leaf through the anthology,
almost unconscious, unaware
I'm counting the dead faces
I've known. Two Roberts—
Hayden & Duncan. Dick
Hugo. Bill Stafford &
Nemerov. Here's Etheridge's
"Circling the Daughter"
again, basic as a stone
dropped into a creek,
a voice fanning out
circles on delta nights.
Anne's haze-eyed blues
at dusk in a bestiary
behind her "reference
work in sin." If we were
ever in the same room,
it isn't for the living
to figure out. Unearthly
desire makes man & woman
God's celestial wishbone
to snap at midnight. Pages
turn on their own & I listen:
Son, be careful what you
wish for. Do I want my name
here, like x's in the eyes
of ex-lovers? I'm thankful
for the cities we drank
wine & talked about swing
bands from Kansas City
into the after hours
under green weather
in this age of reason.

WOEBEGONE

We pierce tongue
& eyebrow, foreskin
& nipple, as if threading wishes
on gutstring. Gold bead
& question mark hook
into loopholes & slip
through. We kiss
like tiny branding irons.
Loved ones guard words
of praise, & demigods mortgage
nighttime. Beneath bruised
glamor, we say, "I'll show
how much I love you by
how many scars I wear."
As we steal the last
drops of anger, what can we
inherit from Clarksdale's blue
tenements? Medieval & modern,
one martyr strokes another
till Torquemada rises.
We trade bouquets
of lousewort, not for the red
blooms & loud perfume,
but for the lovely spikes.

STRANDS

If you had asked
after my fifth highball,
as I listened to Miles' midnight
trumpet, in Venus De Milo's embrace,
I would have nodded
Yes, as if I didn't
own my tongue. *Yes*,
I believe I am
flesh & fidelity
again. I washed lipstick
off the teacup, faced
your photo to the wall,
swept up pieces of goodtime
moshed with dustballs,
& haggled with myself
over a bar of lemon soap.
Yes, I could now feel
luck's bile & desire
sweetened by creamy chocolates,
& I would have bet
my Willie Mays cards
a strand of your hair
clinging to an old Thelonious T-shirt
could never make me fall apart
at this bedroom window
beneath a bloodred moon.

ANODYNE

I love how it swells
into a temple where it is
held prisoner, where the god
of blame resides. I love
slopes & peaks, the secret
paths that make me selfish.
I love my crooked feet
shaped by vanity & work
shoes made to outlast
belief. The hardness
coupling milk it can't
fashion. I love the lips,
salt & honeycomb on the tongue.
The hair holding off rain
& snow. The white moons
on my fingernails. I love
how everything begs
blood into song & prayer
inside an egg. A ghost
hums through my bones
like Pan's midnight flute
shaping internal laws
beside a troubled river.
I love this body
made to weather the storm
in the brain, raised
out of the deep smell
of fish & water hyacinth,
out of rapture & the first
regret. I love my big hands.
I love it clear down to the soft
quick motor of each breath,
the liver's ten kinds of desire
& the kidney's lust for sugar.
This skin, this sac of dung
& joy, this spleen floating
like a compass needle inside
nighttime, always divining

West Africa's dusty horizon.
I love the birthmark
posed like a fighting cock
on my right shoulder blade.
I love this body, this
solo & ragtime jubilee
behind the left nipple,
because I know I was born
to wear out at least
one hundred angels.

UNIVERSITY PRESS OF NEW ENGLAND   publishes books under its own imprint and is the publisher for Brandeis University Press, Dartmouth College, Middlebury College Press, University of New Hampshire, Tufts University, and Wesleyan University Press.

ABOUT THE AUTHOR   Yusef Komunyakaa is a professor in the Council of Humanities and Creative Writing at Princeton University. He is the author of five Wesleyan titles including the Pulitzer-winning *Neon Vernacular* (1993), which also won the Kingsley-Tufts Poetry Award from the Claremont Graduate School; *Magic City* (1992); and *Dien Cai Dau* (1988). In 1991, he won the Thomas Forcade Award, in 1993 he was nominated for the Los Angeles Times Book Prize in Poetry, and in 1997 he was awarded the Hanes Poetry Prize.

ABOUT THE COVER ART
Benjamin West, *Penn's Treaty with the Indians,* 1771-72. Oil on canvas. 75 ½ x 107 ¾". Courtesy of The Museum of American Art of the Pennsylvania Academy of the Fine Arts, Philadelphia. Gift of Mrs. Sarah Harrison (The Joseph Harrison, Jr. Collection)

LIBRARY OF CONGRESS CATALOGING-IN-PUBLICATION ÐATA
   Thieves of paradise / Yusef Komunyakaa.
       p.   cm. — (Wesleyan Poetry)
   ISBN 0-8195-6330-7 (cloth)
   I. Title.   II. Series.
PS 3561.O455T45 1998
811'.54—dc21   97-40294